THE SPIRITUAL SOLDIER, HOLY WARFARE AND THE END OF THE AGE

The Spiritual Soldier, Holy Warfare and the End of the Age

Copyright © 2024 Robert Cowells

All rights reserved.

No part of this publication may be reproduced in a retrieval system, or transmitted in any form or by any means—electronic, mechanical, photocopying, recording, or otherwise—without the prior written permission of the publisher.

A comprehensive list of scripture translation permissions can be found in the backwater of the book with appropriate copyright and publication information.

This manuscript has undergone viable editorial work and proofreading, yet human limitations may have resulted in minor grammatical or syntax-related errors remaining in the finished book. The understanding of the reader is requested in these cases. While precaution has been taken in the preparation of this book, the publisher and author assume no responsibility for errors or omissions, or for damages resulting from the use of the information contained herein.

This book is set in the typeface *Athelas* designed by Veronika Burian and Jose Scaglione.

Paperback ISBN: 979-8-3443-7339-3

Hardcover ISBN: 979-8-3305-9493-1

A Publication of *Tall Pine Books* | Warsaw
www.tallpinebooks.com

| 1 24 24 20 16 02 |

Published in the United States of America

THE SPIRITUAL SOLDIER, HOLY WARFARE AND THE END OF THE AGE

ROBERT COWELLS

I wish to dedicate this book to my friend and brother in Christ, Mark Bryan. Mark and I had a five decade relationship in the bond of the spirit of Jesus Christ. He was my theological buddy. We discussed deeper biblical truths mostly over the phone since we did not live close.

He read my manuscript and provided a very helpful critique. He also encouraged me to publish the manuscript soon and thought it had a timely message. Mark suddenly went to be with the Lord on July 4, 2024. We miss him greatly.

I also wish to dedicate this book to the spiritual soldiers of Christ of my generation, the baby boomers and my grandchildren's generation, gen Z.

Many soldiers of my generation have left the battlefield for their rewards on the other side. Some are still in the battle but not far from completing their good fight of faith. They provide a faithful example for the soldiers of gen Z now coming onto the field of battle. May this current generation of spiritual soldiers of Christ mature quickly and even outshine my generation.

Last but not least I wish to dedicate this book to my fellow soldier of fifty plus years, my wife Sharon. She has faithfully stood by me in every battle especially during the most difficult and darkest days.

THE IMPOSSIBLE DREAM

To dream the impossible dream
To fight the unbeatable foe
To bear, with unbearable sorrow
And to run where the brave dare not go
To right the unrightable wrong
And to love, pure and chaste from afar
To try, when your arms are too weary
To reach the unreachable star
This is my quest, to follow that star
No matter how hopeless
No matter how far
To fight for the right
Without question or pause
To be willing to march into hell
For that heavenly cause

And I know, if I'll only be true

To this glorious quest

That my heart will be peaceful and calm

When I'm laid to my rest

And the world will be better for this

That one man scorned and covered with scars

Still strove with his last ounce of courage

To reach the unreachable

The unreachable

The unreachable

Star

And I'll always dream the impossible dream

Yes and I'll reach the unreachable star

CONTENTS

Introduction	xi
1. Spiritual Warfare	1
2. Our Exalted Supreme Commander and His Evil Nemesis	9
3. The Spiritual Soldier Candidate	17
4. The Soldier's Boot Camp of Character Preparation	27
5. Equipped for Battle – The Full Armor of God	53
6. The United Effort	67
7. Frontline warfare	73
8. The Love of Truth and the End of the Age	77
Epilogue: The Impossible Dream	93
About the Author	95
Permissions	97

INTRODUCTION

This book is intended for those who wish to be serious disciples and spiritual soldiers of Jesus Christ. The truths in this book will help the believer to pursue the narrow way of discipleship and become fully equipped for spiritual warfare. Holiness and humility are key characteristics of those who wish to follow Christ into spiritual warfare.

This book is about both grace and truth; grace cost Jesus Christ everything and comes to us free. Truth will cost us everything, but it is the only way to advance in the Kingdom of God; it is the only way to conform to the image of Christ.

This is no book of band-aids and self-help but is intended to assist the true disciple through the straight gate, down the narrow, difficult way of truth to a deeper knowledge of the resurrection life of Jesus Christ. We need to be fully prepared to follow truth today, tomorrow and, to the end of the age. Only those who love truth will be overcomers of the enemy to the end of the age. Truth in Jesus Christ is the only true defense against the schemes and terrible deceptions of the enemy.

I challenge you to read this book with the intent of embracing the biblical truths found in it. Then to apply them to your life by the grace of God and with the help of the Holy Spirit. As a fully equipped spiritual soldier of Jesus Christ you will be able to defend yourself, to defend the church, and go to battle for others. May He who has begun a good work in you see it to completion.

To those who have not yet surrendered to the lordship of Jesus Christ, He offers you eternal life through the forgiveness of your sins. This is a life of true meaning and great purpose that extends out into eternity, which is forever. This life is available to those who will surrender to Jesus Christ as Lord and Savior.

The Bible reveals to us that all mankind are sinners. We are born that way. We inherit that sin nature from our father Adam. A sinner is not just someone who commits sin but is hopeless and helpless outside of Jesus Christ.

God has taken it upon Himself to resolve the issue of sin by sending His sinless Son to die on the cross in our place. There He paid the price for the penalty of sin. As a result, salvation is now the free gift of God through Jesus Christ our Lord.

Acknowledge yourself a sinner before God, for only a

sinner needs a savior. Cry out to Him for forgiveness through His shed blood. Also submit yourself to the lordship of Jesus Christ. If you do this, you will be born from above and become a child of God. You will then be completely forgiven, washed clean and set free from sin.

Then you can choose to be baptized and receive the gift of the Holy Spirit. Through these decisions, you will be qualified to follow Jesus Christ. As His disciple, your life will take on His great purpose. This will prepare you to read this book and to discover what it is to be a spiritual soldier of Christ.

These two scriptures explain God's gift of salvation:

For by grace you have been saved through faith. And this is not your own doing; it is the gift of God, not a result of works, so that no one may boast. For we are his workmanship, created in Christ Jesus for good works, which God prepared beforehand, that we should walk in them. (Eph 2:8-10 ESV)

"...because if you acknowledge and confess with your mouth that Jesus is Lord [recognizing His power, authority, and majesty as God], and believe in your heart that God raised Him from the dead, you will be saved. For with the heart a person believes [in Christ as Savior] resulting in his justification [that is, being made righteous—being freed of the guilt of sin and made acceptable to God]; and with the mouth he acknowledges and confesses [his faith openly], resulting in and confirming [his] salvation. (Rom 10:9-10 AMP)

TWO PREREQUISITE TRUTHS

Spiritual Versus Natural

It's important to have a basic understanding of the difference between what the Bible calls the natural man and the spiritual man. Knowing the difference will greatly help us in our everyday Christian life and especially being prepared for spiritual warfare.

The natural man is the descendant of Adam, and he inherits Adam's nature which is the nature of sin. Adam in his original creation was a natural man created in the image of God. Once he partook of the fruit of the tree of the knowledge of good and evil, he took on the sin nature of the enemy and corrupted his original nature. The natural man can no longer please God or make any contribution to the Kingdom of God.

God's resolution for the sin-corrupted man was to take the race of Adam to the cross with Jesus Christ. There it was crucified and done away with. Then through His resurrection Jesus Christ as the last Adam becomes the firstborn of a new spiritual race of people in His image.

The only person who can now please God and contribute to the Kingdom of God is the spiritual man born from above. He now belongs to the new humanity created in the image of Jesus Christ. A person becomes spiritual through the new birth. This person takes on the nature of God and becomes alive in his spirit.

The following scriptures will help define the natural and the spiritual.

> *The natural person does not accept the things of the Spirit of God, for they are folly to him, and he is not able to understand them because they are spiritually discerned. (1 Cor 2:14)*

> *Thus it is written, "The first man Adam became a living being"; the last Adam became a life-giving spirit. But it is not the spiritual that is first but the natural, and then the spiritual. The first man was from the earth, a man of dust; the second man is from heaven. As was the man of dust, so also are those who are of the dust, and as is the man of heaven, so also are those who are of heaven. Just as we have borne the image of the man of dust, we shall also bear the image of the man of heaven. (1 Cor 15:45-47)*

Therefore, the normal condition of the born-again believer is spiritual, not natural. The challenge for those who are born from above is to remain in that spiritual condition. We are not to go back and function as natural people out of the sin nature. The believer who attempts to live his life as a natural man out of his own resources and will is called *carnal* in the Scriptures. The church at Corinth demonstrated the destructive outcome of *carnal* Christians. Division was brought to that church through their carnality.

As Christ's followers, we are called to live by faith through the Spirit, thereby maintaining our spiritual position in Christ. We will have a stable spiritual life by continually abiding in Christ. This includes partaking of His living Word and drinking in the living water, which is the Holy Spirit of God.

In these lessons I will give a more detailed description of what it means to be spiritual and what it means to be a spiritual soldier of Christ.

The Precision of God's Word

The Word of God is absolutely precise. God does not waste His words. What He says is exactly what He means. Unfortunately, the Word of God is often handled by preachers and Bible teachers in a very imprecise way. We who teach and preach the Word of God need to be very aware of its exactness. We should proceed with fear and trembling in handling it so that we don't communicate inaccurate information. We need the ministry of the Spirit of Truth when interpreting the Scriptures. He is the only One who knows the true meaning and hidden truths of the Scriptures.

In this scripture, Jesus lets us know there is only one guide to Truth.

> *When the Spirit of truth comes, he will guide you into all the truth... (John 16:13a)*

In this book, I will be careful to honor the preciseness of the Word of God. Some of the truths that I share in this book may challenge certain beliefs you hold. At times the Spirit of truth will attempt to bring correction or enlargement to our paradigm of beliefs. We should constantly with humility present our beliefs to the Holy Spirit for this possibility.

In this book, you may encounter truths that are new to you or counter to some of your current understanding. I would challenge you to prayerfully examine the exactness of the Scriptures for new truth. Truth is a living entity, not just a passive mental belief. The receiving of living truth requires an act of faith on our part. I will give more detailed information on living truth in this book.

I will do my best to respect the preciseness of the Scriptures in this study.

1

SPIRITUAL WARFARE

The spiritual realm cannot be known by the five natural senses. We cannot see it, hear it, touch it, taste it or feel it. It is immaterial. It is only known by faith. There are exceptions to this. There are times when the spiritual realm breaks into the natural realm. We see this in the manifestation of miracles. For example, the feeding of the 5,000 with a few fish and a little bit of bread was a miraculous breaking in of the spiritual domain. The miracles and healings of Christ did not seem to create genuine and permanent faith in the crowds that followed Him. Eventually, they all forsook Him except for His 12 disciples, and even one of them eventually betrayed Him. Our normal relationship with the spiritual sphere is that of faith. We need to develop spiritual senses to function in that realm. Mainly, the spiritual senses of sight and hearing.

Because spiritual warfare happens in the unseen realm, it is easily ignored and even dismissed by some believers. We are natural people born into a natural world and are conformed to it. Therefore, it is a great challenge for believers to enter into the spiritual domain by faith. When a believer from their natural perspective dismisses spiritual warfare as not real, they are deceived by the enemy and cannot have a full and victorious Christian life.

This Bible verse points out the importance of the unseen dimension:

> *So we fix our eyes not on what is seen, but on what is unseen, since what is seen is temporary, but what is unseen is eternal.* (2 Cor 4:18)

Spiritual warfare is directly related to the origin of sin. Lucifer, a guardian cherub of God's throne, exalted himself in pride over his own beauty and rebelled against the *Most High*. Through this sin, a battle of good against evil was initiated. Later, sin was introduced to this world through Adam's fall. By his sin, Adam surrendered the dominion of this earth to Satan, who became the god of this world. In the next chapter, I will give more detail on Satan and sin.

These verses tell us about the evil work of the god of this world, known as Satan:

> *And even if our gospel is veiled, it is veiled to those who are perishing. In their case the god of this world has blinded the minds of the unbelievers, to keep them from seeing the light of the gospel of the glory of Christ, who is the image of God. (2 Cor 4:2-4)*

Because of Adam's fall and Christ's redemption, we are now subject to intense spiritual warfare. There's evidence of spiritual warfare in the Old Testament but it has been greatly intensified in the church age. And that warfare will become even more intense as we approach the end of this age. It is very important that believers be prepared for that warfare today, tomorrow, and, to the end of the age. This book will describe that preparation and the execution of spiritual warfare.

Many times in the Old Testament God is referred to as the Lord of hosts. This can also be translated as the Lord of Armies or the Lord of Angel Armies. Jesus is the commander of these armies of heaven.

> *Lift up your heads, gates!*
> *Be lifted up, ancient doors,*
> *so the King of Glory may come in.*
> *Who is he, this King of Glory?*
> *The L<small>ORD</small> of the heavenly armies—*
> *He is the King of Glory. (Psalm 24:9-10 ISV)*

The Bible doesn't tell us how angels fight. Since angels are spiritual beings with spiritual bodies, they cannot be killed or die. Nevertheless, angels do engage in combat.

In the Old Testament, sometimes angels cross over into the natural realm and exhibit their great power to which human armies are no challenge as described in this verse.

> *And that night the angel of the LORD went out and struck down 185,000 in the camp of the Assyrians. And when people arose early in the morning, behold, these were all dead bodies. (2 Kings 19:35)*

In the book of Daniel, we have information concerning angelic conflict. Also, these scriptures seem to indicate that certain powerful angelic beings, both good and evil, have governmental power over nations. Daniel was in mourning and in prayer concerning the restoration of the Jewish people to Jerusalem. The angel that came to him told him that he attempted to come immediately to Daniel but was hindered for 21 days by an angelic being called the Prince of Persia. Also, the prince of Greece is mentioned along with Michael, the angel over Israel.

> *Then he said to me, "Fear not, Daniel, for from the first day that you set your heart to understand and humbled yourself before your God, your words have been heard, and I have come because of your words. The prince of the kingdom of Persia withstood me*

twenty-one days, but Michael, one of the chief princes, came to help me, for I was left there with the kings of Persia.

Then he said, "Do you know why I have come to you? But now I will return to fight against the prince of Persia; and when I go out, behold, the prince of Greece will come. But I will tell you what is inscribed in the book of truth: there is none who contends by my side against these except Michael, your prince. (Dan 10:12-13, 20-21)

Chapter 12 of the book of Revelation tells us that angelic warfare will continue until the end of this age when the evil one will be cast out of heaven to the earth.

Now war arose in heaven, Michael and his angels fighting against the dragon. And the dragon and his angels fought back, but he was defeated, and there was no longer any place for them in heaven. And the great dragon was thrown down, that ancient serpent, who is called the devil and Satan, the deceiver of the whole world—he was thrown down to the earth, and his angels were thrown down with him. (Rev 12:7-9)

We can take comfort in knowing that angels are called to help the church. Just as they helped the Lord Jesus at times. They came to His aid after His 40 days of fasting. The Bible states they came and ministered to Him. They also helped Him in the garden of Gethsemane. Both times He was close to death.

In the Book of Acts, we know that an angel came and released Peter from prison. Throughout the church age, there have been testimonies of angelic assistance. Based on this verse, I think we can assume they are assisting us even in spiritual warfare.

> *Are not all the angels ministering spirits sent out [by God] to serve (accompany, protect) those who will inherit salvation? [Of course they are!] (Heb 1:14 AMP)*

The church is also called to engage the enemy in spiritual warfare. This warfare is not fought against physical people but against spiritual powers in the unseen realm as indicated in this verse below. These powers appear to be arrayed in a governmental hierarchy. Jesus Himself spoke of the Kingdom of Satan. Only when we function as spiritual soldiers with spiritual weapons will we be effective in this type of warfare.

> *For we do not wrestle against flesh and blood, but against the rulers, against the authorities, against the cosmic powers over this present darkness, against the spiritual forces of evil in the heavenly places. (Eph 6:12)*

Through these scriptures in the book of 2 Corinthians, we see that our minds are a battlefield of this warfare. It is possible to have victory in our minds over every evil, unclean thought and to bring every thought into captivity to the obedience of Christ.

> *For though we walk in the flesh, we are not waging war according to the flesh. For the weapons of our warfare are not of the flesh but have divine power to destroy strongholds. We destroy arguments and every lofty opinion raised against the knowledge of God, and take every thought captive to obey Christ. (2 Cor 10: 3-5)*

The Supreme Victory and its Execution

At the cross, Jesus utterly defeated the enemy and sin. He took back dominion of the earth and became Lord of all. Not only did Jesus die for our sin, but He died to bring back all that the Father had lost through the fall of Satan and the sin of Adam.

These scriptures speak of that victory and Christ's exaltation over all.

> *Forasmuch then as the children are partakers of flesh and blood, he also himself likewise took part of the same; that through death he might destroy him that had the power of death, that is, the devil... (Heb 2:14)*

> *And being found in human form, he humbled himself by becoming obedient to the point of death, even death on a cross.*

Therefore, God has highly exalted him and bestowed on him the name that is above every name... (Phil 2:8-9)

The church is God's primary instrument of warfare on the earth. As the body of Christ, we are His spiritual feet on the ground. He has committed to the church the execution of His victory.

...and what is the immeasurable greatness of his power toward us who believe, according to the working of his great might that he worked in Christ when he raised him from the dead and seated him at his right hand in the heavenly places, far above all rule and authority and power and dominion, and above every name that is named, not only in this age but also in the one to come. And he put all things under his feet and gave him as head over all things to the church, which is his body, the fullness of him who fills all in all. (Eph 1:19-22)

We are His army of spiritual soldiers on the earth. Because we are spiritually seated with Him in the heavenly places, we possess the authority of His throne on the earth to execute His victory over the enemy.

This army is a more glorious army than the host of angels because it has been purchased through His blood and birthed through the cross. **It is an army in His image.** The extent to which this army is conformed to His image will be the extent of its success.

2

OUR EXALTED SUPREME COMMANDER AND HIS EVIL NEMESIS

There are two armies in the battle for good and evil. One is the army of liars and evil led by the supreme liar and murderer. The other is an army of holiness and truth led by Him, the Son of Man, who is truth and holiness. Our army is headquartered in heaven. The army of evil is headquartered in hell. The evil one commands by deceit and intimidation. The Righteous One commands by Grace and Truth.

Let's contrast these two leaders.

Jesus, the Son of Man, earned His position of lordship through the cross and rules over His Kingdom by grace and truth.

And being found in human form, he humbled himself by becoming obedient to the point of death, even death on a cross.

Therefore God has highly exalted him and bestowed on him the name that is above every name, so that at the name of Jesus every knee should bow, in heaven and on earth and under the earth, and every tongue confess that Jesus Christ is Lord, to the glory of God the Father. (Phil 2: 8-10)

Satan gained his authority and Kingdom by deceitfully stealing Adam's dominion over this earth. He rules by deceit and intimidation. Through sin, he holds humanity captive. We believers can give him access to our lives if we persist in sin. Righteousness, holiness and humility will defeat the enemy.

We know that we belong to God even though the whole world is under the rule of the Evil One. (1 John 5:19 GNT)

Through the cross, Jesus has been granted all authority in heaven and on earth and rules from His exalted throne in the heavenlies.

Now the eleven disciples went to Galilee, to the mountain to which Jesus had directed them. And when they saw him they worshiped him, but some doubted. And Jesus came and said to them, "All authority in heaven and on earth has been given to me." (Matt 28:16-18)

Satan is the temporary god of this world system with

restrained authority and power. He can only do what God allows. He is like a dog on a leash. At the end of the age, he will be let off his leash and will be allowed to manifest his full satanic power and deception for a final time. Only those who love the truth will escape this final deception. The love of the truth is the only safeguard against his deceptions today, tomorrow and especially at the end of the age. Only a red-hot love for Jesus Christ can guard us completely against the deceptions of the enemy.

> *The coming of the lawless one is by the activity of Satan with all power and false signs and wonders, and with all wicked deception for those who are perishing, because they refused to love the truth and so be saved. (2 Thess 2:9-10)*

The Bible does not give us a lot of information about the origin of Satan. These two passages of scripture from Isaiah and Ezekiel give us clues as to who Lucifer was and what he became through rebellion against God.

> *"How you are fallen from heaven, O Lucifer, son of the morning! How you are cut down to the ground, You who weakened the nations! For you have said in your heart: 'I will ascend into heaven, I will exalt my throne above the stars of God; I will also sit on the mount of the congregation On the farthest sides of the north; I will ascend above the heights of the clouds, I will be like*

the Most High.' Yet you shall be brought down to Sheol, To the lowest depths of the Pit. (Isaiah 14:12-15 NKJV)

"You were the signet of perfection,
full of wisdom and perfect in beauty.
You were in Eden, the garden of God;
every precious stone was your covering,
sardius, topaz, and diamond,
beryl, onyx, and jasper,
sapphire, emerald, and carbuncle;
and crafted in gold were your settings
and your engravings.
On the day that you were created
they were prepared.
You were an anointed guardian cherub.
I placed you; you were on the holy mountain of God;
in the midst of the stones of fire you walked.
You were blameless in your ways
from the day you were created,
till unrighteousness was found in you.
In the abundance of your trade
you were filled with violence in your midst, and you sinned;
so I cast you as a profane thing from the mountain of God,
and I destroyed you, O guardian cherub,
from the midst of the stones of fire.
Your heart was proud because of your beauty;

> *you corrupted your wisdom for the sake of your splendor.
> I cast you to the ground...(Ezekiel 28:12-17)*

In his original state, Lucifer was full of wisdom and perfect in beauty. Satan still retains wisdom and beauty and can come as an angel of light. Though he still has great wisdom, it is polluted completely by evil and the outcome of his wisdom is only destruction and chaos.

We are no match for his wisdom. Complete dependence on God's wisdom is needed to overcome satanic schemes designed to destroy us. We also are no match for his power. Therefore, we depend on the power of the Holy Spirit in our spiritual warfare.

According to these scriptures, there is a relationship between Lucifer and the Garden of Eden. He is called a guardian cherub. A cherub appears to be a spiritual being higher than the angels. Created to be close to the throne of God, possibly a guardian of the throne.

I think it's possible that Lucifer was God's highest created being and related to worship in heaven.

He had so much influence in heaven that he was able to convince a large portion of the angels to follow him in rebellion against the almighty.

Although Satan was created a beautiful, powerful and wise being, he became infatuated with his own beauty. He desired to have a position equal to God. I believe the position he desired is the position that Jesus Christ, the Son of God, the Son of Man currently holds at the right hand of the Father.

Satan, through his pride and rebellion, is the original sinner. He is the source of sin. Sin is his nature. That poisonous nature was injected into the human race through Adam by his sin.

Satan is a usurper gaining his position by deceitfully stealing it from Adam. He is ferociously jealous of the throne of Christ. Because he cannot dethrone Christ, he seeks to dethrone Him in believers' hearts and local churches.

His tactics against the church include counterfeiting the works of the Holy Spirit. This is witnessed during times of genuine revival and awakenings. This enemy of truth has sought to discredit the gift of the Holy Spirit. Not only by counterfeiting it but by promoting fanaticism connected to the gift of the Holy Spirit. Some believers shun the gift of the Holy Spirit because of the emotional fanaticism promoted by some groups.

By sowing seeds of doubt and fear, he seeks to destroy the faith of believers. By encouraging the self-life, he wishes to bring conflict and disunity to local churches. Through sin in general he wishes to hinder and even destroy holiness in believers and local churches. Ultimately, he wants to bring dishonor to the name of Jesus and hinder His purposes.

But let us remind ourselves that Satan was completely defeated at the cross. He has limited power and authority, and he is as I said earlier, a dog on a leash. He is no equal to

Jesus Christ. He is a created being and Jesus Christ is the uncreated second Person of the Trinity now seated at the right hand of God. He is the Son of Man, our perfect representative before God, our perfect mediator between us and God.

As Joshua led the Israelites to displace the Canaanites in the promised land, so Commander Jesus leads His holy army, the church. This army comes down from heaven to displace Satan and sin, thereby setting the captives free.

These first two chapters lay a foundation for the rest of this study.

3

THE SPIRITUAL SOLDIER CANDIDATE

His calling and qualifications

The true soldier must be chosen and called. The true soldier of Christ does not of his own initiative choose to follow Jesus Christ but surrenders to the calling of God. These verses point out our eternal chosenness.

> *You did not choose me, but I chose you and appointed you that you should go and bear fruit and that your fruit should abide, so that whatever you ask the Father in my name, he may give it to you. (John 15:16)*

> *Blessed be the God and Father of our Lord Jesus Christ, who has blessed us in Christ with every spiritual blessing in the heavenly places, even as he chose us in him before the foundation of the*

world, that we should be holy and blameless before him. (Eph 1:3-4)

To all those in Rome who are loved by God and called to be saints: Grace to you and peace from God our Father and the Lord Jesus Christ. (Rom 1:7)

Christ's soldier and army must be spiritual. Each soldier is born from above. This spiritual new birth causes a person to become a spiritual being and begin to function in the spiritual realm. Only spiritual soldiers with spiritual weapons can effectively engage in spiritual warfare.

In this verse, Jesus tells us there is no spiritual perception apart from the new birth from above.

Jesus answered him, "I assure you and most solemnly say to you, unless a person is born again [reborn from above—spiritually transformed, renewed, sanctified], he cannot see and experience the kingdom of God." (John 3:3 AMP)

Our fleshly, natural birth is through Adam but our spiritual birth is through Christ.

That which is born of the flesh is flesh, and that which is born of the Spirit is spirit. (John 3:6)

The Spirit of Christ is now in the potential soldier, and he has the capacity to see the Kingdom of God but hasn't fully entered the Kingdom. He is in Christ, Christ is in him, and he is spiritually seated with Christ in the heavenlies, the position of authority as this scripture shows.

> *And hath raised us up together, and made us sit together in heavenly places in Christ Jesus... (Eph 2:6)*

He is now a child of God but not yet a soldier.

The Volunteer Army

The newborn believer must volunteer to be a soldier by choosing to follow Christ as Lord and Commander. A soldier is a disciple of Christ.

To be a true disciple/soldier of Christ we must choose to follow Him every day.

> *And he said to all, "If anyone would come after me, let him deny himself and take up his cross daily and follow me. (Luke 9:23)*

The first act in following Christ is water baptism by immersion without delay. This is an act of obedience of discipleship.

We identify with Christ's death, burial, and resurrection through baptism. We leave our old life behind and enter the new, resurrection life of Christ.

Baptism also represents our inner cleansing and clear conscience through the forgiveness of our sins. This prepares us as a temple for our next act of faith. Just as the Old Testament temple had to be ritually cleansed before the presence of God filled it, so we must be spiritually cleansed spirit, soul and body before the Holy Spirit can fill us.

> *And Peter said to them, "Repent and be baptized every one of you in the name of Jesus Christ for the forgiveness of your sins, and you will receive the gift of the Holy Spirit. (Acts 2:38)*

> *Therefore we are buried with him by baptism into death: that like as Christ was raised up from the dead by the glory of the Father, even so we also should walk in newness of life. (Rom 6:4)*

The second act of obedient faith is to receive the gift of the Holy Spirit, which is the soldier's spiritual empowerment. This is the very Person of the Holy Spirit occupying His temple. The enemy greatly fears this empowerment and works his deceit, lies and counterfeits to prevent this empowerment. The enemy has encouraged all kinds of fanaticism connected with the gift of the Holy Spirit to discredit it and to drive sincere believers away from this very needful empowerment.

It is important to understand that the disciples were born from above before the day of Pentecost. John 20:22 tells us that Jesus breathed on them and said to receive the Holy

Spirit or holy breath. In the Greek, the article "the" is not there. He did not breathe on them the Person of the Holy Spirit but His own holy breath.

So, what kind of breath was Jesus breathing on them? The breath was coming from the resurrected Christ; therefore the breath was the spirit of resurrection. And this was their new birth, by the receiving of the spirit of resurrection from Jesus Christ.

As God breathed on Adam, he became the father of the human race, so when Jesus breathed on His disciples, they became the beginning of the new humanity in the image of Jesus Christ. Jesus, the last Adam and the Son of Man, is the firstborn of this new humanity.

As born-again believers, the disciples received the gift of the Holy Spirit on the day of Pentecost. This was their empowerment for service and witness.

These verses speak of the gift of the Holy Spirit which is given to those who ask.

If you then, who are evil, know how to give good gifts to your children, how much more will the heavenly Father give the Holy Spirit to those who ask him!" (Luke 11:13)

...and ye shall receive the gift of the Holy Ghost. For the promise is unto you, and to your children, and to all that are afar off, even as many as the Lord *our God shall call. (Acts 2:38-39)*

This gift of the Holy Spirit is promised for every generation of believers.

The requirements for a soldier's complete salvation according to Jesus and Peter.

> *Jesus replied, "I tell you the solemn truth, unless a person is born from above, he cannot see the kingdom of God." Nicodemus said to him, "How can a man be born when he is old? He cannot enter his mother's womb and be born a second time, can he?" Jesus answered, "I tell you the solemn truth, unless a person is born of water and spirit, he cannot enter the kingdom of God. What is born of the flesh is flesh, and what is born of the Spirit is spirit. Do not be amazed that I said to you, 'You must all be born from above.'" (John 3:3-7 NET)*

Jesus tells us that not only do we need to be born from above to see the Kingdom, but to fully enter into the Kingdom of God we must be born of water and of the spirit. The water speaks of baptism and the spirit refers to the baptism of the Holy Spirit, also known as the gift of the Holy Spirit.

Peter, in his sermon on the day of Pentecost, tells those present the same thing that Jesus said in John 3. That to know salvation they must repent, which brings the new birth. Then they must be water baptized, which prepares them to receive the gift of the Holy Spirit. Our salvation is incomplete without water baptism and the gift of the Spirit.

The new birth makes us His and puts us in Christ for our eternal salvation. But our salvation here and now is incomplete without water baptism and the baptism in the Holy Spirit. The spiritual soldier will be ill prepared to face the enemy without water baptism and the gift of the Holy Spirit.

We must be convinced of the necessity to receive the gift of the Holy Spirit. Until this gift is received, we are not completely prepared to live this Christian life and be a fully equipped spiritual soldier. When we receive the gift of the Holy Spirit, we are immersed without and filled within. We become the temple of the Holy Spirit—spirit, soul and body.

The fire that came on Pentecost with the gift of the Spirit speaks of the sanctifying work of the Holy Spirit. This fire seeks to burn away all that opposes God's holiness in us. The soldier will discover that the first battle to be won is the defeat of sin and self within. The defeat of sin is the beginning of sanctification, not the end. The goal of sanctification is the perfection of holiness. In this context, one of the lies of the Devil is that we must sin. According to the Scriptures, we do not have to sin; sin is always a choice. The work of the cross has provided the deliverance from sin.

Through the work of the cross and the resurrection of Jesus Christ, the Bible says we have a new divine nature within us. And this nature, which is the nature of God, cannot sin. So not only do we not have to sin, but if we walk after this new nature, we cannot sin. So, the challenge and the struggle becomes: Will I walk after the new nature of the

Spirit of God, or will I walk after the old nature of Adam and sin?

> *Whosoever is born of God doth not commit sin; for his seed remaineth in him: and he cannot sin, because he is born of God. (1 John 3:9 KJV)*

> *But I say, walk by the Spirit, and you will not gratify the desires of the flesh. (Gal 5:16)*

Daily we renew our commitment by denying our self-life, taking up our cross (the instrument of death to self and sin) and following Him. We seek to live after the new life and crucify the old life. If we love others, we will not sin against them. Walking after the law of love will keep us from sinning against others.

> *And they that are Christ's have crucified the flesh with the affections and lusts. (Gal 5:24)*

The soldier looks to cooperate with the Holy Spirit's sanctifying work in his life. If we choose to rebel against God and go after sin, the sanctifying fire of the Holy Spirit will greatly intensify. God will seek to draw us back to Himself through His disciplinary actions that can bring true repentance and restoration. Sometimes the Father's discipline can be extremely severe when His child is in rebellion against

Him. This severe discipline may even terminate the life of the believer as was the case with Ananias and Sapphira when they lied to the church and the Holy Spirit (Acts 5:1-10).

The book of Hebrews has much to say about God's discipline. We cannot know His holiness without it.

> *It is for discipline that you have to endure. God is treating you as sons. For what son is there whom his father does not discipline? If you are left without discipline, in which all have participated, then you are illegitimate children and not sons. Besides this, we have had earthly fathers who disciplined us and we respected them. Shall we not much more be subject to the Father of spirits and live? For they disciplined us for a short time as it seemed best to them, but he disciplines us for our good, that we may share his holiness. (Heb 12:7-10)*

Working out our Salvation

> *Therefore, my beloved, as you have always obeyed, so now, not only as in my presence but much more in my absence, work out your own salvation with fear and trembling, for it is God who works in you, both to will and to work for his good pleasure. (Phil 2:12-13)*

We are to work out what God has worked in us. We are not to be only hearers of the Word but also doers. We are God's workmanship. He is working in us to conform us to the image of Jesus Christ. This is His work, not ours. Our job by faith and obedience is to allow what He's doing in us to manifest through us with the help of the Holy Spirit.

> *No one who abides in him keeps on sinning; no one who keeps on sinning has either seen him or known him. Little children, let no one deceive you. Whoever practices righteousness is righteous, as he is righteous. Whoever makes a practice of sinning is of the devil, for the devil has been sinning from the beginning. The reason the Son of God appeared was to destroy the works of the devil. (1 John 3:6-8)*

It is good and necessary that we believe in the imputed righteousness of Christ. We are the righteousness of Christ in God. This is objective spiritual reality. This is how God sees us.

Those who are only intellectual Christians believe doctrinally all the right truths but are not living them out in their lives. Those who are truly following Christ live out righteousness, holiness and the very character of Christ, including love and humility through the grace of God and the power of the Holy Spirit. This is the image of the true spiritual soldier.

4

THE SOLDIER'S BOOT CAMP OF CHARACTER PREPARATION

Being a spiritual soldier of Christ is not an analogy but a spiritual reality. We really can be and should be soldiers of the cross. The church is an actual army under the command of our exalted General.

If we surrender to the Lordship of Christ and choose to follow Him, He will put us into the spiritual boot camp of character formation, which is the image of Christ. Without initial and continuous character transformation, the soldier will be diminished in his ability to overcome the enemy and fulfill God's purpose for himself and the church.

In boot camp, the discipline of all aspects of life will be at the forefront. The soldier is a disciple of Christ. A disciplinarian. The fruit of self-control will begin to grow in this kind of life. We must discipline ourselves in spirit, soul and body.

In this scripture, Paul emphasizes the need to discipline our body.

> *So I do not run aimlessly; I do not box as one beating the air. But I discipline my body and keep it under control, lest after preaching to others I myself should be disqualified. (1 Cor 9: 26-27)*

A spiritual soldier must bring his body and appetites under control. What we eat and how much we eat have a direct effect on our body and health. Carrying extra weight is always detrimental to our health. A lifetime of excessive weight can lead to premature deterioration of the back, hips or knees. Excessive weight almost always contributes to high blood pressure and sometimes heart disease. Excessive sugary carbohydrate intake can greatly affect our cholesterol, Tri glycerol and A1C levels. Over time, this can lead to the development of diabetes and all its negative effects on our bodies.

It should go without saying that the soldier abstains from cigarettes, excessive alcohol and illegal drugs. I highly recommend total abstinence from alcohol. There's little to no benefit in drinking alcohol. In large quantities, it is a poison to our system. The decision concerning alcohol is between you and the Holy Spirit.

Exercise is also very important in the maintenance of our

health. It doesn't have to be a 5k run. Regular walking or biking can be enough.

Because our bodies are the temple of the Holy Spirit, the spiritual soldier chooses to exercise self-control and moderation in his diet and lifestyle. He wishes to present to God daily a body that is fit for the tasks that God has for him.

> *I appeal to you therefore, brothers, by the mercies of God, to present your bodies as a living sacrifice, holy and acceptable to God, which is your spiritual worship. (Rom 12:1)*

The spiritual soldier also exercises self-control over his mind. What we allow ourselves to see and hear is important. Our mind is a battlefield of spiritual warfare. It needs to be spiritually prepared to properly engage and repel the enemy.

In our day, there is easy access to images that don't belong in the mind of the follower of Jesus Christ. The spiritual soldier exercises self-control over what he allows himself to see and hear. This includes the Internet and other visual media such as Hollywood movies.

Pornography is a terrible weapon of the enemy that enslaves many men in our day. This can become an idol in the mind and the heart and can lead to even demonic issues. The spiritual soldier must be totally free from this sinful practice. A believer with an addiction to pornography will probably need assistance from others, which may include prayer for deliverance.

The whole realm of pornography is a great stronghold of Satan. He seeks to promote it and expand it for the sake of bringing great destruction, which includes the breakup of marriages. This realm can be defeated by spiritual soldiers who stand against it by faith, humility and holiness in the power of the Holy Spirit.

The soldier must practice self-control on the Internet and through other media. He needs to avoid inappropriate images and language which pollutes the mind. It is imperative to exclude from our lives websites and programs that we know are inappropriate and will be spiritually damaging to us.

It is very important to not waste the time that God has given us. The spiritual soldier will not waste his time on movies, literature and other activities that don't make a positive contribution to his spiritual life. Even though they are not blatantly sinful.

It is necessary to exercise self-control over social media. An excessive amount of time on social media will not benefit our spiritual life but waste our God-given time. My 20-year-old grandson has begun to regularly fast from social media to assist his spiritual growth. He has also discontinued the use of certain platforms. I commend him for this. This can be very difficult for a young person but very worthwhile.

On the positive side, the Bible tells us what to put into our minds.

Finally, brothers, whatever is true, whatever is honorable, whatever is just, whatever is pure, whatever is lovely, whatever is commendable, if there is any excellence, if there is anything worthy of praise, think about these things. What you have learned and received and heard and seen in me—practice these things, and the God of peace will be with you. (Phil 4:8-9)

The spiritual soldier also pursues spiritual disciplines. These include Bible study, prayer, meditation and quiet times. To pull aside from the noisy world around us and to be still before the presence of God is a necessary practice. This will continually bring new life to our inner being. During these times of stillness, we can feast on the very presence of God. He is our true food. Jesus tells us that unless we eat His flesh and drink His blood, we have no life. His broken flesh and poured-out blood represent what He did for us on the cross. We need to continuously, spiritually eat and drink the finished work of the cross.

Fasting is a spiritual discipline that can assist us in our pursuit after the true knowledge of God. Sometimes God calls us to a period of fasting for a specific purpose in our life or in His Kingdom. Fasting does not have to be for an extended period of time. It can be practiced even in a 24-hour period.

Older people may need to consult with their doctor before going on an extended fast. Fasting can remind us that we are more than physical beings. We truly at our core are spiritual beings through the new birth. Fasting frees up time that we can spend in prayer and quiet meditation.

Churchwide fasts can be a powerful time of spiritual warfare and spiritual advancement for a church.

Fasting is also good for us physically. When combined with drinking plenty of water, it can purge our system of unwanted toxins. Also, it gives our digestive system a rest. This is a way to care for the temple of the Holy Spirit.

No soldier gets entangled in civilian pursuits, since his aim is to please the one who enlisted him. (2 Tim 2:4)

The soldier must handle temporal necessities, but we are not to be entangled in them. They are not to become priorities that overshadow the pursuit of the Kingdom of God.

We are to manage our possessions but not allow our possessions to become a distraction from that which is ultimately our priority, the Kingdom of God.

But seek first the kingdom of God and his righteousness, and all these things will be added to you. (Matt 6:33)

As seekers after the Kingdom of God, we recognize that God is the possessor of heaven and earth. The followers of Christ have no earthly possessions but are called to be faithful stewards of what God allows them to manage. The spiritual soldier does not unnecessarily burden himself with the things of life and the stuff that the world eagerly pursues. We choose to seek the true riches of the Kingdom of God, which includes our relationship with Christ and other believers. These are eternal riches.

The Principle of Death and Resurrection

God's boot camp encompasses all of life. Every day the Spirit will apply the cross to our life in various ways to put the old life to death and bring us more and more into the new life of discipline, humility and holiness. The principle of death and resurrection is woven into the fabric of the entire Bible, both Old and New Testament.

For example, we see it in the life of Joseph. Joseph was the favored son of his father. Joseph had a dream that he would rule over his family. He shared this dream with his mother, father, and brothers. None of them liked his dream. His brothers were enraged by his dream because they were already jealous of him.

They ended up selling him into slavery, which brought to death the dream that Joseph had had. Enslavement and eventual imprisonment were the death of his relationship with his family and past life. For over a decade he was imprisoned where he experienced a double death to his dream and his past life.

But God raised him up and seated him at the right hand of Pharaoh in fulfillment of his dream. In this resurrected position, he was able to save the Egyptians and his family from starvation. This death and resurrection experience also prepared Joseph's character. He became a Christlike person who could properly rule as the second most powerful man in the most powerful empire in the world. Through all his death experiences, Joseph became a humble instrument in the hand of God to fulfill his God-given purpose.

The primary example in the Old Testament of this principle of death and resurrection is the life of Abraham and Isaac.

> *By faith Abraham, when he was tested, offered up Isaac, and he who had received the promises was in the act of offering up his only son, of whom it was said, "Through Isaac shall your offspring be named." He considered that God was able even to raise him from the dead, from which, figuratively speaking, he did receive him back. (Heb 11:17-19)*

God had promised Abraham a son through whom the covenant that God made with Abraham would be fulfilled, even the reality of having an innumerable number of offspring. Abraham had to wait many decades before he saw God fulfill the promise of a son through his barren wife Sarah in their old age.

God tested Abraham by telling him to sacrifice his teenage son, Isaac, on an altar. The scripture indicates that Abraham believed if he carried this out that God would raise

Isaac from the dead. Abraham trusted in the character of God and believed He would not break His promise to fulfill the covenant through his son. This is a powerful demonstration of God's principle of death and resurrection in the life of His servant.

In the New Testament, we see this principle at work in the lives of the 11 disciples when Jesus was crucified and died. All of them had left their jobs and old lives to follow this Messiah. They thought He would overthrow the Romans, set up His Kingdom and they would rule with Him. Their hopes and aspirations died when their Messiah died. They became like dead men with no hope or purpose.

When Jesus rose from the dead, they also were resurrected, and their faith was renewed in the true image of the heavenly Messiah.

In the life of the Apostle Paul, we see this principle probably more severely applied than any other man. His sufferings include blindness, arrest, imprisonment, severe beatings almost to death, shipwreck and being stoned and left for dead. God raised him up out of them all.

Someone once said, "He whom God would use greatly, he must wound deeply." To whom great responsibility is given, great suffering is required.

This scripture points out Paul's high calling as the Apostle to the Gentiles. Jesus also forewarns him of how much he must suffer in relation to this great calling.

> *But the Lord said to him, "Go, for he is a chosen instrument of mine to carry my name before the Gentiles and kings and the children of Israel. For I will show him how much he must suffer for the sake of my name. (Acts 9:15-16)*

This principle will always be active in the life of the disciple-soldier following Jesus Christ. Constantly the Holy Spirit will put to death those things in our lives that hinder us from following Christ. He will replace the things of the old life with the resurrection life of Jesus Christ and further conform us to the very image of Jesus Christ.

Sometimes this principle of death and resurrection will come to us as a fiery, difficult trial that will reduce us to ashes out of which only God can resurrect us, and He will if we remain faithful.

I have seen this principle of death and resurrection at work in my life from the very beginning of my Christian walk.

I encountered Jesus Christ during the Jesus movement of the early 1970's. This movement was a sovereign act of God that brought multitudes of teenagers and young adults into the Kingdom of God.

I met Jesus in December of 1971 in a small Pentecostal church in St. Clair Shores, Michigan. This small church had opened its doors to the movement of the Spirit among the long-haired, bearded, bell-bottomed, freaky kids. Many of these young people were trying to escape a meaningless life of drugs, alcohol and rock and roll.

Even though I looked the part, out of respect for my parents, I refrained from drugs. But I drank beer daily, and a few weeks after my conversion on my 21st birthday, I had a terrible hangover. I decided the Lord wished me to abstain from alcohol, which I have to this day.

Some friends who were new believers invited me to this small church on a weekday night.

As I walked into that church, there were freaky-looking kids setting up their musical instruments, which included guitars and drums. This was long before it became common for churches to have worship bands. I commend the leadership of that small church who went out of their way to bring these kids to Christ.

In this church, I sensed a different atmosphere than I had ever experienced before. I would call it the atmosphere of holiness, and my silent prayer the whole time was, "Lord make me like these people." The Bible tells us that no one can call Jesus Lord except by the Holy Spirit, and I believe that happened to me that night.

An older female pastor brought the message that night. I was so distracted by the sense of holiness and my inner crying out to God that I didn't really hear any of the message. At the very end, she invited whoever would like to ask Jesus into their heart to raise their hand. I thought everybody was going to raise their hand. As I began to raise my hand, it felt like an invisible hand came down and pulled my hand all the way up.

At the same time, I was powerfully immersed in the presence of a holy God. I surrendered to this presence. I started to weep like a baby as I felt a terrible sorrow for my sins. I felt a tremendous burden of shame lifted from me; a burden I didn't know I had been carrying. I sensed I was forgiven, and a sense of holiness entered me.

This was my first experience of death and resurrection. The Bible says that before we know Christ we are dead in our sins and trespasses. As a 20-year-old, I felt hopeless, helpless and without purpose in life. The enemy tries to give people a sense of meaning to life outside of Jesus Christ. I did not have that false sense, and I was very blessed for that. When I came to Christ, I suddenly had a sense of great purpose and of destiny in Christ. I was now experiencing His resurrection life.

That first year of my Christian life was a great struggle for me. Within a couple of months of my initial salvation, I joined a Baptist Church and was baptized. I began to come under the teaching of the doctrine of salvation. I felt that I had not understood or fulfilled any of these requirements of the doctrine of salvation. My salvation experience had been an encounter with an invisible God without real understanding in my mind of the gospel of Jesus Christ. This caused a lot of doubt and confusion. I wasn't sure I had met the requirements of salvation.

Later, I found out through the Scriptures that He chooses us, we don't choose Him. Probably the best word to use is that we surrender to His choosing of us.

I began to enter an extended time of doubt, confusion and even despair. I could not decide whether I was really saved. I was constantly praying the sinner's prayer but had no assurance that I truly had salvation. This went on for many months. I was in a state of darkness, depression and confusion. I am sure the enemy had his hand in this. He wished to destroy my newfound faith in Christ.

Eventually, I came across a scripture in the book of Hebrews, chapter 11, verse six. It states that he who comes to God must believe that He is and that He's a rewarder of those who diligently seek Him. I told God I was confused about my salvation, but I believed in Him and with all that lay within me, I would seek Him with my whole heart.

From that day forward, by faith I stood on the Word of God and believed that I had salvation and began to seek Him with my whole heart.

My initial encounter with Jesus was a powerful experience of spontaneous repentance and forgiveness with little to no understanding of who this God was. Months later, I found my salvation confirmed through His living Word to me in Hebrews 11. This was the first scripture God wrote on my heart. It was a living truth for me.

The more I read the Scriptures, the more I came to understand that my salvation was of Him and not of me. The

Bible says in First Corinthians, chapter one that by God's doing we are in Christ Jesus. When some people come to Christ, they have a good understanding of the gospel, but others not so much and some hardly at all. That's God's choice of how He brings us to Himself. Our salvation is not in the gospel message but in the One to whom the message points. It is not enough to agree with the gospel message. We must obey it by surrendering to the Lordship of Jesus Christ.

After being in darkness and confusion for several months, God raised me up out of that death and planted my feet on the solid ground of His salvation. The apex of this experience of His resurrection life was receiving the gift of the Holy Spirit and being powerfully immersed in the Spirit.

In the coming decades, I would experience some very severe spiritual death experiences that reduced not only me to ashes but also my wife. The enemy not only wanted to destroy my faith but also our family, which includes three children. Out of all these fiery trials, God raised us up and planted our feet on resurrection ground. He will do the same for you. Always remember that things don't just happen in our lives. Either God causes them, or He allows them, but the Scriptures tell us in Romans 8:28 that He causes all things to work together for good to those who love Him and are called according to His purpose.

He doesn't cause all things, but He will bring good out of all things and cause His purpose to be advanced in our lives if we are following Christ as His disciples. These death experiences are the outworking of the cross by the Holy Spirit to cause death to the old and bring forth the new in Jesus Christ. Our experiences of death and resurrection will vary in severity. On a scale of one to ten, not every experience will be as severe as a ten, but every trial will potentially advance us spiritually in the Kingdom of God.

Every true soldier-disciple of Jesus Christ will experience this principle of death and resurrection many times over in their lifetime. This is the only way to Christian maturity. This is the straight gate, the narrow and difficult path that leads to life in Jesus Christ, resurrection life.

The Father's Discipline

One of the ways of God to bring us to maturity and spiritual fruitfulness is the heavenly Father's discipline. It is the only way to holiness.

His discipline helps to keep us on the straight and narrow way. When we veer off the way and pursue sin, His discipline will help to bring us back to where we should be. Then we can continue the pathway of holiness. Anyone who can walk away from the Lord and does not suffer the discipline of our loving Father never belonged to Him in the first place. The Bible says if you are without discipline, you're not His child.

> *God is treating you as sons. Is there a son whom his father does not discipline? Now if you are without any discipline, in which*

all sons share, then you are illegitimate and not God's sons. (Heb 12:7-8)

The Father also disciplines us when we're doing well. This is like the pruning of a grapevine. The caretaker of the vineyard at the end of a season will cut back good branches and leave the vine looking almost dead. This is done so that the next season the pruned vine will bring forth even more fruit.

Sometimes the difficulties we go through, the dark times we go through are orchestrated by God to bring forth more fruit from our lives. To take away good that He might bring forth the best.

Also, we do not wish to be an undisciplined, wild grapevine. When I was a young teenager, my father planted a grapevine behind our house which was just outside of my bedroom window. It was supported by horizontal wires that were attached to vertical posts.

In a field about 50 or 60 feet behind that grapevine was a wild grapevine growing up a supporting cable of a telephone pole.

The grapevine started at ground level and went up about 20 or 30 feet in the air to the telephone pole and hung like a huge curtain of leaves. This wild grapevine only produced very small green grapes that were not edible. It was very unfruitful. But it looked rather impressive compared to my father's grapevine, especially after it was pruned.

My dad's grapevine through pruning was continually confined to the area of his fencing. The wild grapevine was free to grow at will over a large area. I believe there is a spiritual principle of confinement through spiritual pruning that is God's way of bringing forth the best fruit.

An undisciplined Christian and even an undisciplined ministry can look impressive, but is it bringing forth God's fruit? It is a wild grapevine that may look impressive to the natural eye but is only producing wood, hay and stubble (1 Cor 3:11-15). Some of these self-serving, unauthorized wild grapevines, so-called Christian ministries, may undergo a severe judgment at the seat of Christ.

> *Not everyone who says to me, 'Lord, Lord,' will enter the kingdom of heaven, but the one who does the will of my Father who is in heaven. On that day many will say to me, 'Lord, Lord, did we not prophesy in your name, and cast out demons in your name, and do many mighty works in your name?' And then will I declare to them, 'I never knew you; depart from me, you workers of lawlessness.' (Matt 7:21-23)*

All the activities of those who are rejected could have been performed before an audience. Their performance was for self-exaltation. All those who are commended before the Lord did good works that were done in secret, not on a stage. These were for the eyes of God, not for the eyes of men.

> *Then the King will say to those on his right, 'Come, you who are blessed by my Father, inherit the kingdom prepared for you from the foundation of the world. For I was hungry and you gave me food, I was thirsty and you gave me drink, I was a stranger and you welcomed me, I was naked and you clothed me, I was sick and you visited me, I was in prison and you came to me.' Then the righteous will answer him, saying, 'Lord, when did we see you hungry and feed you, or thirsty and give you drink? And when did we see you a stranger and welcome you, or naked and clothe you? And when did we see you sick or in prison and visit you?' And the King will answer them, 'Truly, I say to you, as you did it to one of the least of these my brothers, you did it to me.'*
> (Matt 25: 34-40)

The pruned grapevine can look almost like a dead vine. It does not look very impressive. But it will produce more and better fruit in its season.

I believe the Apostle Paul is a great example of what happens when God prunes a productive Christian life and ministry. For much of his Christian ministry, Paul was free to travel the known world of that time and plant churches and even revisit them and help to establish them.

At the end of his life, Paul was arrested and confined to imprisonment. This looked as if his ministry was over and his productivity for the Kingdom of God had come to an end. But through this time of pruning, even this time of confinement, Paul wrote letters that later became many of the epistles of the New Testament. Paul went from a highly productive Christian ministry across the world into a prison of confinement. Here he produced even more fruit that remains to this day, which we call his prison epistles of the New Testament.

So be encouraged, soldier, when you find yourself in a place of confinement by the pruning of God. In that place, God is cutting away the good to bring forth His best. This can be a painful experience but produces eternal results.

The Bible also says that God the Father scourges every son that He receives. This is the same word that is used to describe the torture that Jesus underwent when being beaten by a Roman soldier with a whip. It contained pieces of glass and metal that would tear away the flesh.

This spiritual scourging is the most extreme form of God's discipline.

I don't know if this happens with every believer, but it definitely happens for some believers. I think it is especially applied to followers of Christ who are being given very weighty responsibilities. Through God's severe means, He prepares the character of those who would accomplish great responsibilities. Joseph in the Old Testament and Paul in the New Testament are examples of this severe discipline.

Not every soldier in God's army will go through these deeper times of discipline. Probably every true leader in the army will have to go through deeper discipline. This prepares them for the responsibilities of leadership. These leaders are called elders in the New Testament.

> *And ye have forgotten the exhortation which speaketh unto you as unto children, My son, despise not thou the chastening of the Lord, nor faint when thou art rebuked of him: For whom the Lord loveth he chasteneth, and scourgeth every son whom he receiveth. If ye endure chastening, God dealeth with you as with sons; for what son is he whom the father chasteneth not? (Heb 12:5b-7 KJV)*

Some believers probably don't recognize God's hand of discipline. They blame it on the devil, circumstances or other natural causes. And because of this, at times they may push the discipline away and not allow God to have His full way with what He wishes to accomplish.

Unfortunately, zealous believers and zealous leaders at times will pray against God's disciplinary work in a person's life. Sometimes God's discipline in a person's life is even attributed to the work of the devil. It is very dangerous to attribute the work of God to the work of the devil. This can bring spiritual disaster.

God's way of discipline can take on many forms, including illnesses, certain losses, including the loss of a job and relational difficulties. Not all forms of discipline such as sickness come directly from the hand of God. But under His sovereignty, He will allow these things into our lives and use them for our good and His purpose. He will also use them to get our attention, especially when we veer off the narrow way.

> *And we know that in all things God works for the good of those who love him, who have been called according to his purpose. (Romans 8:28 NIV)*

> *But strait is the gate and narrow and difficult is the way that leads to life, and there are few who find it. (Matt 7:14 combined KJV and AMP)*

> *Confirming the souls of the disciples, and exhorting them to continue in the faith, and that we must through much tribulation enter into the kingdom of God. (Acts 14:22 KJV)*

If we choose to deny our self-life (strait gate) and take up our cross (narrow and hard way), He will lead us to ever-deepening infusions of His life. This is the only way into a deeper experience of the Kingdom of God, truth and true Christian maturity. The narrow way is the spiritual birth canal that pushes us out into new life. If we are faithful followers, He will repeat this spiritual process all our lives. This is the biblical principle of death and resurrection woven into all the Bible.

To get anything of value out of life requires a great deal of effort. To become a successful doctor, lawyer or engineer requires many years of great effort educationally and on the job. To have a lifelong marriage requires a great effort on the part of both partners. To get a relatively small amount of gold out of the ground requires a costly investment in equipment and man hours. For God to get spiritual gold out of our lives will require a lifetime of His work in us and a cooperating effort on our part. That which has value does not come cheaply or easily. The strait and narrow, the way of the cross, is the only way to a life that is pleasing in God's sight. Satan will offer easy shortcuts around the cross and pseudo-spiritual formulas that only accomplish a man-made, poor imitation of the true Christian life, which will lead to defeat and even despair.

> *...continue to work out your salvation [that is, cultivate it, bring it to full effect, actively pursue spiritual maturity] with awe-inspired fear and trembling [using serious caution and critical self-evaluation to avoid anything that might offend God or discredit the name of Christ]. For it is [not your strength, but it is] God who is effectively at work in you, both to will and to work [that is, strengthening, energizing, and creating in you the longing and the ability to fulfill your purpose] for His good pleasure. (Phil 2:12b-13 AMP)*

> *By the grace God has given me, I laid a foundation as a wise builder, and someone else is building on it. But each one should build with care. For no one can lay any foundation other than*

> the one already laid, which is Jesus Christ. If anyone builds on this foundation using gold, silver, costly stones, wood, hay or straw, their work will be shown for what it is, because the Day will bring it to light. It will be revealed with fire, and the fire will test the quality of each person's work. If what has been built survives, the builder will receive a reward. If it is burned up, the builder will suffer loss but yet will be saved—even though only as one escaping through the flames. (1 Cor 3:10-15)

The spiritual soldier chooses the hard way of the cross rather than the easy way that leads to destruction and death. We go this way because we love Him who chose the hard way of the cross on our behalf.

God's discipline will humble us and keep us humble. Some may say a good father would not intentionally hurt their child. If a child is so ill that they require surgery to save their life, what good father wouldn't submit their child to the pain of surgery? Our heavenly Father will submit us to spiritual surgery at times. Sometimes very severe spiritual surgery is required to save our spiritual lives.

Trained in Truth

The Boot Camp of Character Preparation includes training in truth. The faithful soldier will continually seek to be instructed in truth by the Spirit of truth. This is his food as the Holy Spirit is his drink. The Spirit's classroom is all of life.

Truth is a living entity that is implanted into our hearts by the working of the Spirit of truth. Doctrine only benefits us at the intellectual level, but truth is engrafted into our innermost being where it brings transformation. We must go deeper than just a superficial doctrinal understanding of the Scriptures. Through the Spirit of truth, we can dive deep into the vast ocean of biblical truth hidden beneath the surface. Truth is like hidden treasure only found by those who diligently hunger, thirst and seek for it.

> *Therefore, ridding yourselves of all filthiness and all that remains of wickedness, in humility receive the word implanted, which is able to save your souls. (James 1:21)*

> *When the Spirit of truth comes, he will guide you into all the truth... (John 16:13)*

> *Sanctify them in the truth; your word is truth. (John 17:17)*

Through the ministry of the Spirit of truth the soldier will come to an ever-deepening true knowledge of who Christ is and who we are in Him. As the soldier allows truth to take hold in him, his faith in the true image of God will deepen and his ability to overcome the enemy will expand.

But grow in grace, and in the knowledge of our Lord and Saviour Jesus Christ. To him be glory both now and for ever. Amen. (2 Peter 3:18)

The new birth and the gift of the Holy Spirit will give the soldier a strong desire for truth. This is the true knowledge of Jesus Christ by which he will grow spiritually. The desire for truth will be maintained as we pursue a personal relationship with the Lord that includes the discipline of prayer and quiet times. Also, the Lord can lead us to those pastors, teachers and authors who can feed us spiritually. Growth in the knowledge of truth requires the practice of truth. Being doers of the Word. The knowledge and love of the truth not only transforms us but is the ultimate defense against the lies, deceptions and counterfeits of the enemy. At the end of the age, only those who love the truth will stand against the final deception.

5

EQUIPPED FOR BATTLE – THE FULL ARMOR OF GOD

In the time of Christ, Roman soldiers wore a specific kind of armor, held a sword and a very large shield, almost head to toe. The Apostle Paul would have been very familiar with the Roman soldier's armor since he was guarded by Roman soldiers while he was in captivity at the time that he wrote the book of Ephesians.

Putting on the armor of God is putting on Christ; it is putting on the new man created in His image. To successfully engage in spiritual warfare, we must put on the full armor of God.

> But put on the Lord Jesus Christ, and make no provision for the flesh, to gratify its desires. (Rom 13:14)

And that ye put on the new man, which after God is created in righteousness and true holiness. (Eph 4:24)

Here in Ephesians, the putting on of Christ is broken down into pieces of spiritual armor.

Finally, be strong in the Lord and in the strength of his might. Put on the whole armor of God, that you may be able to stand against the schemes of the devil. For we do not wrestle against flesh and blood, but against the rulers, against the authorities, against the cosmic powers over this present darkness, against the spiritual forces of evil in the heavenly places.

Therefore take up the whole armor of God, that you may be able to withstand in the evil day, and having done all, to stand firm. Stand therefore, having fastened on the belt of truth, and having put on the breastplate of righteousness, and, as shoes for your feet, having put on the readiness given by the gospel of peace. In all circumstances take up the shield of faith, with which you can extinguish all the flaming darts of the evil one; and take the helmet of salvation, and the sword of the Spirit, which is the word of God, praying always with all prayer and supplication in the Spirit, and watching thereunto with all perseverance and supplication for all saints.. (Eph 6:10-18)

Let me break this section of scripture into smaller pieces and give my best interpretation.

(Vs 11) Put on the whole armor of God, that you may be able to stand against the schemes of the devil.

We must be strong in His strength. Our strength of personality, intellect or gifts does not count in this warfare. Only when we are daily Spirit-infused through death and resurrection will we count. Put on the whole armor, not part, to defeat the enemy's schemes to steal, kill and destroy.

The enemy's nature and schemes

The thief comes only to steal and kill and destroy. I came that they may have life and have it abundantly. (John 10:10)

His schemes include putting doubt in our hearts toward God. As he successfully did with Eve when he asked her, "Hath God said?" Is God good and trustworthy?

The enemy tempts us in many ways to follow after the old man, our old nature of sin. Ultimately, the enemy wishes to dethrone Christ in our lives and enthrone self and sin. Each piece of armor protects us in a specific way from the schemes of the enemy. Each piece of armor is a living principle of truth to be received by faith.

Our spiritual wrestling

(Vs 12) For we do not wrestle against flesh and blood, but against the rulers, against the authorities, against the cosmic powers over this present darkness, against the spiritual forces of evil in the heavenly places.

In ourselves, we have no power against these cosmic powers of evil. The battle is in the spiritual realm, and we have little to no understanding of this realm. We need the wisdom and power of God to operate there. We need to be in the Spirit.

(Vs 13) Therefore take up the whole armor of God, that you may be able to withstand in the evil day, and having done all, to stand firm.

Three times the word "stand" appears in verses 11-13. We stand our ground upon the finished work of the cross. The armor is defensive. We defend what Christ has done for us and who we are in Him. We especially need to be prepared for the evil day when the enemy comes against us in an especially severe way.

The first piece of armor:

(Vs 14) Stand therefore, having fastened on the belt of truth–

The belt is one of the first pieces of armor an ancient soldier put on. It holds his weapon and breastplate in place. The belt holds the sword.

Truth is mentioned first. Without truth, the armor has no spiritual value and is useless against the enemy. No truth, no victory. The Word of God (sword of the Spirit) is always related to truth and vice versa. We are to be totally wrapped in the belt of truth—spirit, soul and body.

The belt was also a soldier's identification and status. The enemy knows by our belt of truth whether we are a threat. He is not intimidated by mere doctrinal knowledge. He is driven back by the manifestation of living truth in the soldier's life, which includes authority in the name of Jesus.

Every piece of armor is related to a principle of truth concerning an aspect of our salvation.

Second piece of armor:

(Vs 14b) and having put on the breastplate of righteousness,

For our sake he made him to be sin who knew no sin, so that in him we might become the righteousness of God. (2 Cor 5:21)

The righteousness of Christ is imputed to us at salvation. By God's action based on Christ's sacrifice, we are placed in Christ. We surrender our sins and receive His righteousness.

By faith, we stand on this truth against the false accusations of the enemy.

The breastplate includes the assurance of our salvation. Without assurance, the enemy can convince us we do not belong to Christ.

God sees us as He sees His Son because our life is hidden in God in Christ. We must know deeply that we have a right standing with God through the righteousness of Christ. We are in Christ by God's doing.

And because of Him you are in Christ Jesus, who became to us wisdom from God, righteousness and sanctification and redemption... (1 Cor 1:30)

To know that God has put us in Christ gives us great confidence before the enemy. We are who we are in Christ by God's work and His grace. By faith, we stand on these great truths.

His righteousness is also imparted to us at the new birth. Christ in us, our hope of glory.

To defeat the enemy, we must live out this righteousness.

Little children, let no one deceive you. Whoever practices righteousness is righteous, as he is righteous. (1 John 3:7)

The third piece of armor:

> *(Vs 15) and, as shoes for your feet, having put on the readiness given by the gospel of peace.*

With shoes on, we are ready to stand our ground or march. The Roman soldiers' footwear had metal cleats hammered into the bottom that helped to give them sure footing on any kind of terrain. Peace with God gives us sure footing because we know we are on His side, and He is on ours. He is our commander, and we are His soldiers. With these shoes, we may march into new spiritual territory that is dark and confusing, but we have peace and confidence that God is for us.

> *What shall we then say to these things? If God be for us, who can be against us? (Rom 8:31)*

> *The God of peace will soon crush Satan under your feet. The grace of our Lord Jesus Christ be with you. (Rom 16:20)*

Also, we carry the gospel of peace to those captive in sin and enemies of God.

> *How beautiful upon the mountains are the feet of him who brings good news, who publishes peace, who brings good news of*

happiness, who publishes salvation, who says to Zion, "Your God reigns." (Isaiah 52:7)

The fourth piece of armor:

(Vs 16) In all circumstances take up the shield of faith, with which you can extinguish all the flaming darts of the evil one;

Faith always has as its object as Jesus Christ and His Word. By faith, we are able to hold up truth against every accusation and temptation of the enemy.

Our faith can extinguish the flaming darts before they can cause a spreading fire of destruction. Such as a flaming sexual temptation. If succumbed to, it could result in the fiery destruction of a marriage, family, or church.

A flaming dart of temptation to spread gossip can end in widespread destruction in a congregation. Through the truth of God's Word, we understand the destructiveness of sin and therefore resist it by the shield of faith. We also resist the darts of the enemy because we don't wish to bring dishonor to the name of Jesus. Through the shield of faith, we quench the enemies of doubt and fear.

If any of you lacks wisdom, let him ask God, who gives generously to all without reproach, and it will be given him. But let him ask in faith, with no doubting, for the one who doubts is like a wave of the sea that is driven and tossed by the wind. For that person must not suppose that he will receive anything from the Lord; he is a doubleminded man, unstable in all his ways. (James 1:5-8)

Through humility and submission to God, we resist the devil, and he will flee.

"God opposes the proud but gives grace to the humble." Submit yourselves therefore to God. Resist the devil, and he will flee from you. Draw near to God, and he will draw near to you. (James 4:6b-8a)

In battle, a group of Roman soldiers would join their shields together at times to protect each other. When the church comes together in unified prayer and praise in Jesus' name, she can raise up a powerful unified shield of faith against the enemy.

The fifth piece of armor:

(Vs 17) and take the helmet of salvation,

This helmet protects our minds from false teachings, doubts and accusations about our salvation by embracing the truths of our salvation. We must be grounded and rooted in these truths. This includes that our salvation is all of Him, not of us.

We need to know that God put us in Christ, not ourselves. He is the craftsman who is producing the image of Christ in us and through us. We cooperate with this work by faith and obedience. We also cooperate with this great work by living out the good works that God has created for us to do.

For by grace you have been saved through faith. And this is not your own doing; it is the gift of God, not a result of works, so that no one may boast. For we are his workmanship, created in Christ Jesus for good works, which God prepared beforehand, that we should walk in them. (Eph 2:8-10)

We stand on the truth that our salvation is secure in Him.

For I am persuaded, that neither death, nor life, nor angels, nor principalities, nor powers, nor things present, nor things to come, nor height, nor depth, nor any other creature, shall be able to separate us from the love of God, which is in Christ Jesus our Lord. (Rom 8:38-39)

The Roman soldier's helmet protected him against the blows of the enemy. The helmet of salvation can protect us from the enemy's blows that can cause despair, hopelessness, and depression. Sometimes these feelings of darkness can come over us, but we don't have to let them overcome us. We remember and stand on the truths of our salvation. We also need to practice perseverance during these dark times.

Having hope and knowing that God's deliverance is a sure thing but will come in His time.

> *But let us, who are of the day, be sober, putting on the breastplate of faith and love; and for an helmet, the hope of salvation. (1 Thess 5:8)*

> *He who has begun a good work in you will perfect it unto the day of Christ. (Phil 1:6)*

> *To appoint unto them that mourn in Zion, to give unto them beauty for ashes, the oil of joy for mourning, the garment of praise for the spirit of heaviness; that they might be called trees of righteousness, the planting of the LORD, that he might be glorified. (Isaiah 61:3)*

The sixth piece of armor:

> *(Vs 17b) and the sword of the Spirit, which is the word of God.*

This last piece speaks of the living Word of God through the Spirit of Truth. We want to take up the Spirit's sword, not ours. Not our ideas or logic but His living Word.

> *For the word of God is living and active, sharper than any two-edged sword, piercing to the division of soul and of spirit, of joints*

and of marrow, and discerning the thoughts and intentions of the heart. (Heb 4:12)

Jesus Himself used the living Word to repel the enemy. He did not engage the enemy with logical or rational arguments, but He simply quoted the Word of God in the power of the Spirit.

Then Jesus was led up by the Spirit into the wilderness to be tempted by the devil. And after fasting forty days and forty nights, he was hungry. And the tempter came and said to him, "If you are the Son of God, command these stones to become loaves of bread." But he answered, "It is written, 'Man shall not live by bread alone, but by every word that comes from the mouth of God.'" Then the devil took him to the holy city and set him on the pinnacle of the temple and said to him, "If you are the Son of God, throw yourself down, for it is written," 'He will command his angels concerning you, and 'On their hands they will bear you up, lest you strike your foot against a stone.'" Jesus said to him, "Again it is written, 'You shall not put the Lord your God to the test.'" Again, the devil took him to a very high mountain and showed him all the kingdoms of the world and their glory. And he said to him, "All these I will give you, if you will fall down and worship me." Then Jesus said to him, "Be gone, Satan! For it is written, 'You shall worship the Lord your God and him only shall you serve.'" Then the devil left him, and behold, angels came and were ministering to him. (Matt 4 1-11)

This is the only piece of armor that is both defensive and offensive. When God sends us on the offensive at the enemy, we need to be prepared to use the living Word of God. We don't use human reason and logic against the enemy. We speak the Word through the Holy Spirit. In conjunction, we use the authority of Christ by His name. And we know we have His authority because the Scriptures say we are seated with Him in the heavenly places.

(Vs 18) *Praying always with all prayer and supplication in the Spirit*

Prayer is our primary method of warfare. Especially corporate prayer. The church has great authority and power when gathered in His name. His name represents the finished work of the cross and the Spirit of His holiness. The church's corporate prayer in Jesus' name is much more powerful than the individual's prayer.

The church's corporate prayer must be spiritual and will only be spiritual when we pray in the full meaning of Jesus' name.

To be clothed in the full armor of God means that we stand by faith on the finished work of the cross, and we are empowered by the Spirit of holiness. Humility and love are chief characteristics of being fully prepared. The spiritual soldier fully equipped like this will be successful in spiritual warfare.

6

THE UNITED EFFORT

Warfare is not waged by individuals but by units of soldiers properly prepared, united in purpose and committed to one another. Deep bonds can be created when soldiers go into combat. This is true in spiritual warfare. As spiritual soldiers pray together and for one another, the bond of love is deepened.

> Mark 6:7: *And he called unto him the twelve, and began to send them forth by two and two; and gave them power over unclean spirits...*
>
> Luke 9:1-2: *Then he called his twelve disciples together, and gave them power and authority over all devils, and to cure diseases. And he sent them to preach the kingdom of God, and to heal the sick.*

Luke 10:19: Behold, I have given you authority to tread on serpents and scorpions, and over all the power of the enemy, and nothing shall hurt you.

The local church is Christ's basic unit of united warfare. We are united by the Spirit as one body and share a common vision and goal. Our bond is His love. Our vision is to gather in the lost, see believers brought to maturity and see the church prepared for the coming of Christ, a church without spot or wrinkle.

Rom 8:29: For those whom he foreknew he also predestined to be conformed to the image of his Son, in order that he might be the firstborn among many brothers.

1 Cor 12:13: For in one Spirit we were all baptized into one body—Jews or Greeks, slaves or free—and all were made to drink of one Spirit.

The church is charged with enforcing His victory by faith and obedience. Our empowerment is the Holy Spirit, and our authority is directly related to the church's holiness. Sin in the church will diminish our authority over the enemy and even totally nullify it. Sin gives the enemy a foothold in our lives and in the church. We must be free from sin to be successful in spiritual warfare. As the body of Christ, we are

His boots on the ground here on earth. The Head is in heaven, commanding the body on the earth.

> *Eph 1:20-23: ...that he worked in Christ when he raised him from the dead and seated him at his right hand in the heavenly places, far above all rule and authority and power and dominion, and above every name that is named, not only in this age but also in the one to come. And he put all things under his feet and gave him as head over all things to the church, which is his body, the fullness of him who fills all in all.*

Leaders of God's Army

The local unit is made up of foot soldiers and leaders. The leaders are called elders. All go through spiritual training, but the leaders' training will be more severe to prepare them for their task. Leaders must exhibit humility and love toward Christ and His church. Leaders must maintain the unity of the Spirit in the bond of peace and always recognize that the church is a holy entity born of God and come down from heaven.

Without humility, the leader will be ineffective and divisive. True leaders will undergo God's humbling ways. Moses, in order to be qualified to lead the nation of Israel, went through decades of humbling experience, including 40 years away from the nation serving as a shepherd of sheep before he shepherded Israel. The Bible calls him the humblest man that ever lived.

The greater the responsibility given to a leader, the deeper the humility required.

The leaders must allow the Holy Spirit to lead. Soldiers must allow the leaders to lead through their God-given authority. An army cannot function apart from submission to authority. Otherwise, there would be disorder and even chaos. Leadership and direction come down from heaven, not up from below. Church leaders must be sure that their plans are God's plans. Only those plans that come down from above will have God's approval and God's success.

Sin in the church will give Satan a foothold. Especially rebellion against leadership, which is a very serious offense against the Lord as these scriptures show.

> *Now Korah the son of Izhar, the son of Kohath, the son of Levi, with Dathan and Abiram the sons of Eliab, and On the son of Peleth, sons of Reuben, took men; and they rose up before Moses with some of the children of Israel, two hundred and fifty leaders of the congregation, representatives of the congregation, men of renown. They gathered together against Moses and Aaron, and said to them, "You take too much upon yourselves, for all the congregation is holy, every one of them, and the LORD is among them. Why then do you exalt yourselves above the assembly of the LORD?" (Numbers 16:1-3)*

> Now it came to pass, as he finished speaking all these words, that the ground split apart under them, and the earth opened its mouth and swallowed them up, with their households and all the men with Korah, with all their goods. So they and all those with them went down alive into the pit; the earth closed over them, and they perished from among the assembly. Then all Israel who were around them fled at their cry, for they said, "Lest the earth swallow us up also!" And a fire came out from the LORD and consumed the two hundred and fifty men who were offering incense. (Numbers 16:31-35)

> For rebellion is as the sin of witchcraft, And stubbornness is as iniquity and idolatry. Because you have rejected the word of the LORD, He also has rejected you from being king." (1 Samuel 15:23)

The Holy Conduit

The church is God's holy conduit upon the earth to transmit God's will from heaven to earth. The Head in heaven transmits His will through His body, the church, upon the earth.

> Verily I say unto you, Whatsoever ye shall bind on earth shall be bound in heaven: and whatsoever ye shall loose on earth shall be loosed in heaven. Again I say unto you, That if two of you shall agree on earth as touching any thing that they shall ask, it shall be done for them of my Father which is in heaven. For where two

or three are gathered together in my name, there am I in the midst of them. (Matt 18:18-20 KJV)

The local church's primary method of warfare is spiritual worship and prayer by a holy army properly prepared and empowered. When the enemy comes against us, he needs to find nothing in us that is of his Kingdom, specifically sin. To the extent he finds sin in the church is the extent to which he will have authority over us and defeat us.

If the church uses the ways and means of the world to conduct its ministries, this will diminish and possibly completely nullify its spiritual power and influence. A church built on and managed by the ideas and wisdom of man is an earthly imitation of the true church come down from heaven. It can make no contribution to the Kingdom of God.

To the extent the church stands on the finished work of the cross and manifests the holiness of Christ, will be the extent of its success in spiritual warfare.

7

FRONTLINE WARFARE

Every day, we soldiers of the cross stand on the finished work of the cross by faith and obedience. We eat the truth and drink in the Spirit. We acknowledge the righteousness of Christ and pursue holiness. We humbly serve others. We maintain our defensive position in the full armor of God with spiritual prayer.

On certain occasions, God may call us to the front lines to take up an offensive position against the enemy. We must be called to this by the Holy Spirit and not take it upon ourselves. A soldier never goes into frontline combat on his own initiative. He must be sent. Without Jesus' authority and power, we will be soundly defeated and even severely, spiritually wounded.

These scriptures show the disciples, the original spiritual

soldiers, being sent into frontline warfare. They went with Jesus' power and authority.

> *Then he called his twelve disciples together, and gave them power and authority over all devils, and to cure diseases. And he sent them to preach the kingdom of God, and to heal the sick. (Luke 9:1-2)*

We must encounter the enemy in a unit of at least two or three who go in His name under the cross. Often, this can be like hand-to-hand combat (we wrestle not against flesh and blood) with only leaders involved but with the backing of the prayers of the church.

> *And he called unto him the twelve and began to send them forth by two and two; and gave them power over unclean spirits... (Mark 6:7)*

Satanic attacks can be most intense during and following a special visitation of the Holy Spirit. In the past, these visitations of the Holy Spirit included the Great Awakenings of the 18th and 19th centuries and times of revival like the visitation upon Wales in 1904.

During spiritual preaching and worship, large numbers of Christians were mightily revived, and multitudes of the lost were powerfully converted. During these times, the enemy will attempt to disrupt the move of God. Part of the enemy's intent is to turn attention from the genuine to his counterfeits, sometimes leading to fanaticism. He will introduce false teachings. Some of these the bible calls doctrines of demons. Spiritual preaching and teaching supported by prayer are a strong weapon against the enemy in these special times.

He will try to deceive with false manifestations of the Holy Spirit to disrupt the receiving of the gift of the Holy Spirit. He will try to discredit the working of God with lies and falsehoods spread by those opposed to the work of God. Usually, the greatest opposition came from some leaders in the established church who opposed the new work of God in these revivals.

The demonic may be manifested during these times. There may be opportunity to cast out demons and heal the sick. During times of genuine revival and awakenings, there were always these kinds of satanic attacks. Often the workings of Satan were not recognized and immediately countered. The Welsh revival of 1904 was stifled and discredited by these unrecognized activities of the enemy.

Will God send widespread revival and awakening again? Will we recognize it as genuine, be prepared to receive it, defend it and preserve it through biblical discipleship? Some leaders in the church think that God will send one more widespread revival in preparation for the end of the age.

We don't have to wait for a large-scale revival; we can

have personal revival now. Most of these steps to personal revival come from the Welsh revival.

1. Surrender to God totally. The Holy Spirit may identify some areas of your life that need to be surrendered.
2. Forsake all sin and anything questionable. Take action to remove any avenue of temptation. Exercise self-control.
3. Be baptized if you never have been. You are not a disciple until you have been baptized.
4. Receive the gift of the Holy Spirit. Become convinced from Scripture that this is a legitimate gift. By faith, receive this gift and leave any experience up to God's choosing. Do not seek an experience; only seek after God.
5. Pursue truth and holiness. Do not conform to any standards of the world. Be willing to stand alone for truth. Hunger and thirst for Christ.
6. If you haven't already, join a holy, God-fearing, Bible-believing church.

This is the way to be prepared to stand against the enemy today, tomorrow and unto the end of the age.

8

THE LOVE OF TRUTH AND THE END OF THE AGE

These scriptures tell us what to expect at the end of the age before the coming of Christ. I will tell you how to be prepared.

Concerning the coming of our Lord Jesus Christ and our being gathered to him, we ask you, brothers and sisters, not to become easily unsettled or alarmed by the teaching allegedly from us—whether by a prophecy or by word of mouth or by letter—asserting that the day of the Lord has already come. Don't let anyone deceive you in any way, for that day will not come until the rebellion occurs and the man of lawlessness is revealed, the man doomed to destruction. He will oppose and will exalt himself over everything that is called God or is worshiped, so that he sets himself up in God's temple, proclaiming himself to be God. Don't you remember that when I was with you, I used to tell you these things? And now you know what is holding him back, so that he may be revealed at the proper time. For the secret power of lawlessness is already at work; but the one who now holds it back will continue to do so till he is taken out of the way. And then the lawless one will be revealed, whom the Lord Jesus will overthrow with the breath of his mouth and destroy by the splendor of his coming. The coming of the lawless one will be in accordance with how Satan works. He will use all sorts of displays of power through signs and wonders that serve the lie, and all the ways that wickedness deceives those who are perishing. They perish because they refused to love the truth and so be saved. For this reason God sends them a powerful delusion so that they will believe the lie and so that all will be condemned who have not believed the truth but have delighted in wickedness. (2 Thess 2:1-12)

For false messiahs and false prophets will appear and perform signs and wonders to deceive, if possible, even the elect. So be on your guard; I have told you everything ahead of time. "At that time people will see the Son of Man coming in clouds with great power and glory. And he will send his angels and gather his elect from the four winds, from the ends of the earth to the ends of the heavens. "But about that day or hour no one knows, not even the angels in heaven, nor the Son, but only the Father. Be on guard! Be alert! You do not know when that time will come. It's like a man going away: He leaves his house and puts his servants in charge, each with their assigned task, and tells the one at the door to keep watch. "Therefore keep watch because you do not know when the owner of the house will come back—whether in the evening, or at midnight, or when the rooster crows, or at dawn. If he comes suddenly, do not let him find you sleeping. What I say to you, I say to everyone: 'Watch!'" (Mark 13: 22-37)

Concerning the end of the age and the return of Jesus Christ, the Bible tells us explicitly here that no man knows the day or the hour but only the Father. The emphasis in Mark 13 is that we are to watch with an exclamation point. That we're not to be those who are asleep at the coming of Christ. To be asleep is to be unaware of what is going on spiritually around us. It is to be focused on and caught up with those things that distract us from the Kingdom of God. The priorities of the Kingdom of God are not to be supplanted by secondary concerns.

The Bible gives us enough information here to help us know that the hour is approaching. Second Thessalonians tells us that before the coming of Christ the man of sin, the lawless one, also known as the Antichrist, will be revealed. It also says that he will no longer be restrained; he will be the dog let off his leash. He will be able to unleash his full satanic power against this world.

We can't know all the details of the coming of the lawless one nor does anyone have a complete understanding and interpretation of the Book of Revelation. I believe as we get closer to the end of the age that the Spirit of truth will reveal more and more of the true meaning of the Book of Revelation. It will not be to satisfy those who are curious but to prepare and strengthen those who wish to take a stand against the enemy and for truth. These are those who wish to overcome, even to the laying down of their lives.

In like manner, every day we are to lay down our lives by denying our self-life, taking up our cross (the instrument of death to the self-life) and following Him wherever He leads. Those who embrace this life of self-denial and following Christ will be prepared for whatever the future brings.

And they overcame him by the blood of the Lamb, and by the word of their testimony; and they loved not their lives unto the death. (Rev 12:11)

With the information we have here in these two sets of scriptures and other information in the Bible concerning the character of Satan, we can anticipate at least in part how the age will end with this unveiling of the evil one.

As Jesus Christ is the true God of truth and reality, the enemy, the evil one, is the false god of lies and unreality. As reality is the outward manifestation of truth, at the end of the age unreality will be the manifestation of the ultimate and final lie. Many believers will be confused by the manifestations of unreality and will need to cling to the Truth in Jesus to be overcomers.

The lawless one will be allowed to manifest great power through signs and wonders that will give credence to his lie. People will be led to believe that this person must be God since he manifests such tremendous power and remarkable signs and wonders. These false manifestations may be a part of a false, counterfeit Christianity. The enemy never creates something original but always copies that which is of God in counterfeits.

> *The coming of the lawless one is by the activity of Satan with all power and false signs and wonders, and with all wicked deception for those who are perishing, because they refused to love the truth and so be saved. Therefore God sends them a strong delusion, so that they may believe what is false, in order that all may be condemned who did not believe the truth but had pleasure in unrighteousness. (2 Thess 2: 9-12)*

Today there are those who crave supernatural manifestations and experiences. This can open the door to the deceptions of the enemy. What we seek is the Kingdom of God and His righteousness. This carnal desire for the supernatural will continue to the end of the age and will contribute to the great deception.

For the lawless one to come and rule this world proclaiming himself to be God, the world must be made ready. The evil ways that are going on in our world today are a preparation for his coming. The way is being prepared for the ultimate lie and deception through the current distortions of truth and promotion of unreality.

Many government leaders around the world resort to lies and distortions to promote their agendas. True Christianity will more and more come under persecution and be seen as the enemy of the state. The end of the age may be like the beginning of the church age with tremendous persecution but now assisted by modern technology.

There are already the beginnings of a convergence of government, science (including artificial intelligence), medicine, computer technology and financial controls that will eventually set the stage for the rule of the evil one. Also, before the end, we will see a new unified religion that will embrace the lie and proclaim it as truth.

The antichrist needs a world system through which he can manifest absolute control over the masses. This would include the development of the mark of the beast. We don't know for sure what this mark will be, but it may be a part of the technological ability of the beast to monitor people wherever they are. The receiving of this mark may be voluntary at first and then become mandatory with repercussions for those who resist. The Book of Revelation tells us that one repercussion for those who will not receive the mark is that they will be prevented from buying and selling. This could be accomplished through governments that set up a digital currency system.

The truth is that the evil one is coming and he's coming

with lies, deception and counterfeits. His purpose is to exalt himself as god over this world. The people of the world will blindly fall in line to worship the beast and give allegiance by gladly receiving the mark of the beast for whatever benefit is promised. They will drink the Kool-Aid!

The Bible says that the very elect of God will be tempted to believe this enticing lie that the enemy will bring into our world. If believers embrace truth within and without, and rely on God's strength and the power of the Holy Spirit, they will be able to endure unto the end.

At the end of the age, this world will be thrown into a type of mass psychosis where people will fully enter into Satan's unreal world. They will be completely detached from God's reality. This is somewhat true now. People of the world lie in the power of the evil one.

First John 5:19 says, *We know we are from God, and the whole world lies in the power of the evil one (CEB)*.

The world believes the lies of the enemy, including that life has meaning outside of Jesus Christ. The world pursues all manner of sinful idols to find meaning and fulfillment, but they all end in destruction and death. They live in the unreal world of relative truth. They believe the enemy's lies in various forms.

They refuse to love the truth. At the end of the age, the Bible says that God will send these people a strong delusion that they might believe the ultimate lie and be damned. When the world is totally plunged into the unreality of the

Kingdom of Satan, the true church will stand in stark contrast as it manifests the reality of the Kingdom of God.

The Bible tells us that anyone can escape this evil world system of darkness by surrendering to the Lordship of Jesus Christ and be transferred into the Kingdom of light and have eternal life.

> *Who hath delivered us from the power of darkness, and hath translated us into the kingdom of his dear Son... (Col 1:13)*

How will believers resist this coming deception and stand up to that unreal world? The Bible says in Thessalonians that those who will be deceived are those who do not love the truth. The only absolute defense against the deception and the lies of the enemy is the love of truth. That is true now, that is true tomorrow and that will be true at the end of the age.

A part of our job as believers and churches is to help prepare the next generation to face whatever it is that God allows to come against that generation. If every generation is able to successfully prepare some to be faithful and true in their generation, then God will have a faithful remnant at the end of the age. The Bible calls that discipleship. And we cannot disciple anybody else unless we ourselves are disciples, even spiritual soldiers. If we love the truth, we will live the truth and be able to share the truth with others in word and deed, helping them to be built up in the faith.

What does it mean to love the truth?

> John 14:6: *Jesus saith unto him, I am the way, the truth, and the life...*

> John 14:15: *If ye love me, keep my commandments.*

> Eph 6:14: *Stand therefore, having your loins girt about with truth, and having on the breastplate of righteousness...*

> 3 John 4: *I have no greater joy than this: to hear that my children are living according to the truth (CEB).*

Jesus Christ is the truth, and only with a personal relationship with the truth, that is with Him, will we truly know truth at the heart level. He tells us if we love Him, we'll keep His commandments. His commandments are the entire Bible. We are to embrace all the truths of Scripture that God reveals to us. We are to walk in the light revealed to us so that we may continually receive more light from the Spirit of truth.

The foundational piece of the spiritual soldier's armor is truth, the belt of truth. Each piece of armor is a spiritual principle of truth. When we are fully clothed in the armor of God, including the sword of the Spirit and the shield of faith, we will be a soldier who can stand against the deception, lies and power of the enemy. This is by the grace of God and the power of the Holy Spirit.

To truly love the truth is to have a heartfelt, heart-level desire for Jesus Christ, who is the truth. A red-hot love for Jesus Christ will always keep us in the narrow way of truth. We must maintain this love and not allow it to grow cold.

Neither are we to be lukewarm, which is a mixture of hot and cold. God hates mixture. In the Old Testament, the Jewish people often tried to mix idol worship with the true worship of Jehovah. This is called syncretism. This mixture of hot, which is the worship of Jehovah, and cold, which is the worship of idols, eventually brought God's judgment and destruction of Israel, which ended in their captivity in Babylon.

New Testament believers are not to imitate this by bringing in the philosophy and ways of the world into our thinking or into our churches. We need to constantly allow the Holy Spirit to purify our hearts and minds with the truth.

We also need to allow the Holy Spirit to lead the church in truly heavenly and spiritual ways, not the ways of the world. Only that which comes down from heaven by prayer will produce the fruit God is looking for. Good ideas coming up from man will only produce wood, hay and stubble, not the silver, gold and precious stone that will endure the testing fire of God.

> *Now if anyone builds on the foundation with gold, silver, precious stones, wood, hay, straw—each one's work will become manifest, for the Day will disclose it, because it will be revealed by fire, and the fire will test what sort of work each one has done. (1 Cor 3:12-13)*

We are not to be conformed to this world's way of living, but we are to be transformed by God's truth through the Spirit of truth into the very image of Jesus Christ. Truth will touch every area of the disciple's life. This only happens with our cooperation of faith and obedience. Those who are being transformed by truth, which is also called sanctification, will shine ever brighter as the world gets ever darker. Those who walk in truth are never deceived by the enemy's lies.

> *I appeal to you therefore, brothers, by the mercies of God, to present your bodies as a living sacrifice, holy and acceptable to God, which is your spiritual worship. Do not be conformed to this world, but be transformed by the renewal of your mind, that by testing you may discern what is the will of God, what is good and acceptable and perfect. (Rom 12: 1-2)*

When the US Secret Service trains agents to recognize counterfeit money, they don't study counterfeit bills but only study genuine bills. In like manner, the more thoroughly we are trained in truth, the more easily we will recognize the enemy's counterfeits. We don't need to study evil to recognize evil. In fact, we need to be careful not to fill our minds with the images and details of evil that come through the media. This can appeal to and stir up the carnal nature. This information is only pollution in our minds and has no spiritual value. Our minds are to be a holy dwelling place of the thoughts of God. The Holy Spirit in His sanctifying work seeks to transform our minds into a holy, pure and tranquil place of worship.

Through the work of the Holy Spirit, our inner life can become like a sea of glass before the throne of God. A place of absolute tranquility. John Wesley called this inner transformation complete sanctification. Our job is to maintain what the Spirit does in us. One of the ways we do this is to prevent the pollution of the world from entering our minds. Because we cannot always prevent this, we need a constant cleansing of the Word of God by the Holy Spirit. We are to be wise as serpents and innocent as doves. We are to think about what is honest, just, pure, lovely, things of good report and anything virtuous.

> *Behold, I am sending you out as sheep in the midst of wolves, so be wise as serpents and innocent as doves. (Matt 10:16)*

> *Finally, brethren, whatsoever things are true, whatsoever things are honest, whatsoever things are just, whatsoever things are pure, whatsoever things are lovely, whatsoever things are of good*

report; if there be any virtue, and if there be any praise, think on these things. (Phil 4:8)

Seekers of Truth

We are not to be just readers of the Bible, but we are to be seekers after the truth. We are to hunger and thirst after truth. God only gives His living water to the truly thirsty. We are to be seekers after the hidden truths of the Scriptures.

The Bible is like a bottomless, boundless ocean of truth to be discovered only by the revelation of the Spirit of truth. It is like hidden treasure that is discovered only by the diligent and obedient seeker. Truth is food and drink for the spiritually hungry and thirsty. Intellectual belief in the mind, the embracing of doctrine, is not the same as the heart-level embracing of truth. Doctrine is only of spiritual value when it is an expression of our knowledge of truth at the heart level.

Truth is a living entity and is to be implanted into us, bringing transformation into the image of Jesus Christ. Doctrine has its place of importance, but again, only as it relates to truth. The scribes and Pharisees were terrible examples of men who knew doctrine and teaching. In fact, they knew the Old Testament very well. To be a Pharisee, you had to memorize the first five books of the Bible and sometimes the whole Old Testament. They knew Scripture, but they did not know truth.

When they encountered Him who is the truth, they opposed Him and became His primary enemy. To know doctrine only is spiritual death. The Apostle Paul says that the letter alone kills, but the Spirit gives life. Only the Spirit of truth brings the words of the Bible alive to us. Doctrine alone can produce self-righteous, religious people who neither know God nor love their fellow man, as was the case with the Pharisees and scribes.

> *Therefore put away all filthiness and rampant wickedness and receive with meekness the implanted word, which is able to save your souls. (James 1:21)*

The Local Church

To live truth fully, we must be a part of a local church. Many of the commands of the New Testament are only lived out in the fellowship of a local church. Chief among them is to love one another through which the world will know He is real, and we are His disciples.

> *...if I delay, you may know how one ought to behave in the household of God, which is the church of the living God, a pillar and buttress of the truth. (1 Tim 3:15)*

> *A new commandment I give unto you, That ye love one another; as I have loved you, that ye also love one another. By this shall*

all men know that ye are my disciples, if ye have love one to another. (John 13: 34-35)

The church, the true church, is like an ark of safety in the midst of a world system under the wrath of God like the days of Noah. Today's ark, like Noah's ark in his day, is also under construction. The construction is the work of the Holy Spirit through the cooperation of the church to bring in and disciple new believers that make up this spiritual ark.

Jesus did not die to save this world system. He died to save people from this world system. Our job as the church is to bring in those who will come and to disciple them in truth so that they might lead spiritually fruitful lives that honor Jesus Christ. The church is like a mighty army with spiritual soldiers who stand to defend the holy ark, defend truth as it is in Jesus Christ and help disciple those who will come into the holy ark of safety today, tomorrow and to the end of the age.

Jesus, the Lord and Savior, is the doorway into the ark. To those outside of the ark, we say come, surrender to Jesus Christ, and receive Him as Lord and Savior. Come quickly into the ark of salvation and safety.

To those who are in the ark of safety, continue in truth, stand against the enemy, and persevere in the face of tribulations, even to the end of the age.

EPILOGUE: THE IMPOSSIBLE DREAM

Our great Salvation not only forgives our sins, for which we are eternally grateful, but also gives us an unbelievably great purpose and destiny that extends out into eternity. The Bible tells us we're being conformed to the very image of Christ, and we're being prepared to be rulers with Christ for all eternity. This is like a dream. This is like an impossible dream. The truth of the matter is that it is impossible. We cannot start our salvation, we cannot continue our salvation, and we cannot consummate our salvation apart from He who began a good work in us and will finish it. Our job is to follow Him by faith and obedience.

You soldiers of the cross, both men and women, I encourage you to continue to live out this impossible dream and to pursue this dream to the very end.

May zeal for the Lord by the Holy Spirit propel you to the finish line.

To those of you who are older soldiers with battle scars within or without, may you finish this quest more gloriously than when you began it. To you younger soldiers, be sure to follow the example set by the older soldiers who have been faithful in this quest of the Kingdom of God.

He who testifies to these things says, "Surely I am coming soon." Amen. Come, Lord Jesus! (Rev 22:20)

ABOUT THE AUTHOR

Robert Cowells has been a zealous follower of Jesus Christ since 1971. He had a powerful encounter with Jesus during the Jesus movement of that era. He has been teaching the Bible for over five decades mostly in a small Baptist Church in Roseville, Michigan. During most of that time he has served as a Deacon. He and his wife Sharon celebrated their 50th wedding anniversary recently. They have 3 married children and 5 grandchildren.

PERMISSIONS

Unless otherwise noted, all scripture quoted in The Holy Bible, English Standard Version® (ESV®) Copyright © 2001 by Crossway, a publishing ministry of Good News Publishers. All rights reserved. ESV Text Edition: 2016.

Scripture taken from the New King James Version®. Copyright © 1982 by Thomas Nelson. Used by permission. All rights reserved.

Scripture quotations from The Authorized (King James) Version. Rights in the Authorized Version in the United Kingdom are vested in the Crown. Reproduced by permission of the Crown's patentee, Cambridge University Press.

Scriptures taken from the Holy Bible, New International Version®, NIV®. Copyright © 1973, 1978, 1984, 2011 by Biblica, Inc.™ Used by permission of Zondervan. All rights reserved worldwide. www.zondervan.com The "NIV" and "New International Version" are trademarks registered in the United States Patent and Trademark Office by Biblica, Inc.™

Scripture quotations taken from the Amplified® Bible (AMP), Copyright © 2015 by The Lockman Foundation. Used by permission. www.lockman.org.

The Scriptures quoted are from the NET Bible® https://netbible.com copyright ©1996, 2019 used with permission from Biblical Studies Press, L.L.C. All rights reserved.

www.ingramcontent.com/pod-product-compliance
Lightning Source LLC
LaVergne TN
LVHW042251070526
838201LV00105B/300/J